DK Life Stories

Nelson

MANDELA

DK Life Stories

Nelson MaNDeLA

by Stephen Krensky

Illustrated by Charlotte Ager

Senior Editors Marie Greenwood, Allison Singer, Roohi Sehgal
Senior Designer Joanne Clark

Editor Kritika Gupta
Art Editor Kanika Kalra
Jacket Coordinator Issy Walsh
Jacket Designer Dheeraj Arora
DTP Designers Sachin Gupta, Ashok Kumar
Picture Researcher Aditya Katyal
Pre-Producer Sophie Chatellier
Producer Amy Knight
Managing Editors Laura Gilbert, Monica Saigal
Deputy Managing Art Editor Ivy Sengupta
Managing Art Editor Diane Peyton Jones
Delhi Team Head Malavika Talukder
Creative Director Helen Senior
Publishing Director Sarah Larter

Subject Consultant Dr Matthew Graham
Literacy Consultant Stephanie Laird

First published in Great Britain in 2019 by
Dorling Kindersley Limited
80 Strand, London, WC2R 0RL

Copyright © 2019 Dorling Kindersley Limited
A Penguin Random House Company
10 9 8 7 6 5 4 3 2
002–314132–July/2019

A CIP catalogue record for this book
is available from the British Library.
ISBN: 978-0-2413-7791-8

Printed and bound in China

A WORLD OF IDEAS:
SEE ALL THERE IS TO KNOW

www.dk.com

Dear Reader,

Nelson Mandela was a man of his time. How could he not be? There was no way for him to ignore the challenging circumstances of his childhood and young adult years. Born into a deeply prejudiced South Africa in 1918, he grew up to witness first-hand his country's official apartheid policy.

And yet he was a man whose actions transcended his own time as well. His enemies released him in 1990 after 27 years of imprisonment. At such a moment, many leaders in his position would have sought revenge under the guise of justice.

But not Nelson. What did he do instead? He showed a remarkable capacity for forgiveness, a willingness to put the past aside and concentrate on the future. As he stated so clearly, "If you want to make peace with your enemy, then you have to work with your enemy. Then he becomes your partner."

Nelson Mandela bravely teamed up with the white South Africans that had kept the black population under their thumbs for so long. In doing so, he both saved his country and set an example to the world.

Stephen Krensky

The life of...
Nelson Mandela

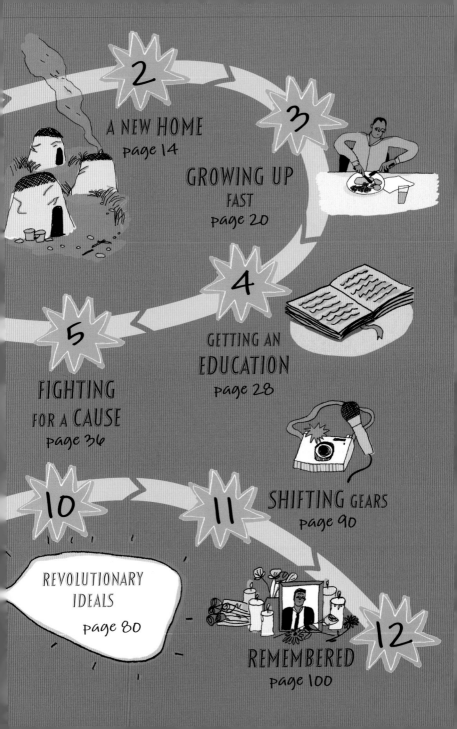

Chapter 1

Troublemaker

**On the day Nelson Mandela was born –
18 July 1918 – his name was not Nelson.
That name would come later.**

At birth, his father gave him the name
Rolihlahla (khol-ee-HLAA-hlaa). Its literal
meaning is "pulling the branch of a tree", but
informally it means "troublemaker". Nobody
claimed that the name was a sign of things to
come – but nobody said it wasn't, either.

Rolihlahla's father, Gadla Henry Mandela,
was a member of the royal house of the Thembu
tribe. His job was advising
people and he was well
respected for his opinions.
Baby Rolihlahla lived with
his mother, Nosekeni Fanny,
in Mvezo (oohm-VEH-zoh).

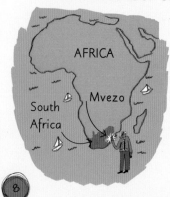

AFRICA

South
Africa

Mvezo

Mvezo was a village on the Mbashe River. It lay deep in the Transkei, a land of gentle hills and shallow valleys 965 km (600 miles) from the big South African city of Johannesburg.

The Mbashe River winds through the Transkei area.

Their home in Mvezo was called a kraal. A kraal is a small farm, with just a few animals and crops, that could support a single family. Rolihlahla's father saw him at the kraal regularly, but for only a few days at a time. Gadla Henry's responsibilities often took him away from home. He had three other wives and many other children to care for. Rolihlahla was the youngest of his four sons, which did not make him very important.

DID YOU KNOW?

Afrikaans, the language of South Africa today, is mostly Dutch, with some differences in vocabulary and grammar.

At the time the native people of South Africa were part of the British Empire. Dutch colonizers had first arrived in South Africa in 1652, and they had not come just to visit. Instead, they had come to settle, and they spent the next 150 years fighting with local tribes until they finally achieved control over the region.

However, their victory was short-lived. In the 1800s, soldiers and pioneers from Great Britain aggressively settled in South Africa. This led to a series of wars that finally ended with a British victory in 1902. Eight years later, South Africa was granted some independence – but it remained in the British Commonwealth, under the firm control of British and Dutch descendants.

What are colonizers?

People who create a new settlement in a foreign land. Colonizers of South Africa created settlements without caring what the native people thought.

CLASH OF THE COLONIZERS

The Anglo-Boer War was a war of independence fought between the Dutch descendants in South Africa and the British Empire that ruled them. It began in 1899 and ended with a British victory in 1902.

British troops ride into battle during the Anglo-Boer War.

The British and Dutch control over South Africa included control over the land's native people. Where could they live? What education could they receive? Which jobs could they have? These issues were harshly regulated. Certain jobs gave some people power over their fellow black Africans, but no jobs gave black people authority over their white neighbours.

Little Rolihlahla knew none of this, of course. Even so, the outside world soon intruded on his own life. When he was barely a year old, his father got into a heated disagreement with a local white magistrate. The complaint itself was small – something about an ox – but Gadla Henry made an issue of it by defying the magistrate's order that he

look into it. Gadla Henry was a member of his tribe's royal family, a descendant of kings. He felt that a mere magistrate should not be able to order him around.

Gadla Henry may have been right in his belief, but he paid dearly for his views.

What is a magistrate?

A government official who administers certain laws in a specific area. The magistrate in Gadla Henry's town was strict.

Black men, even descendants of kings, held power only with the permission of the all-white government. The members of that government did not like seeing their authority challenged. The magistrate dealt harshly with Gadla Henry, taking away much of his land and fortune. This decision sent a clear message to anyone who might share his views.

Among the possessions the magistrate took away was the kraal where Rolihlahla and his mother lived. Under the existing laws, they had no right to argue with this decision. All they could do was move.

2

A new home

Rolihlahla's family needed a new home, and they didn't have to look far. Gadla Henry still owned some property, including a kraal in Qunu.

It was a nearby village, home to only a few hundred people. It was smaller than Mvezo, but the land was much the same, with grassy fields and hills fed by bubbling streams.

Gadla Henry's kraal in Qunu consisted of three domed mud huts with thatched roofs. One hut was used to sleep in, and the other two were for cooking and storing food. The floors of the huts were made of crushed "ant-heap", which is the hard dirt above an ant colony. Rolihlahla's family used fresh cow dung to keep the floors smooth. There was a hole in the roof for cooking smoke to escape through. The only way in or out of each hut was a low doorway.

None of the huts had any wooden furniture. Everyone slept on mats. Outside, there were fields to grow crops and pens for the farm animals. The kraal was not fancy, but it was a comfortable place to live and it allowed Rolihlahla's family to be self-sufficient.

In the nearby fields, Rolihlahla learned to use a slingshot. Like many boys his age, he became skilled enough to shoot birds out of the sky. Later in life, he remembered learning "to gather wild honey and fruits and edible roots, to drink warm, sweet milk straight from the udder of a cow... and to catch fish with twine and sharpened bits of wire."

What does "self-sufficient" mean?

Being able to survive on your own. Because Rolihlahla's family grew their own food on the kraal, they were self-sufficient.

Besides fishing and gathering food, Rolihlahla played games, too. The most popular was called *thinti*. Rolihlahla also spent time mastering the art of stick fighting. This was a kind of swordplay that featured thrusts and parries, feints and lunges. All the while the participants danced back and forth as nimbly as they could.

Rolihlahla liked the time he spent exploring the land and playing games with his friends, but his parents knew he had a quick mind, worthy of great achievements. They could not read or write, but his mother wanted Rolihlahla to do both, so they decided to send him to school.

PLAYING THINTI

Thinti was a game that featured two sticks that were used as targets about 30 m (100 ft) apart. Two teams of boys would each defend their target while trying to throw sticks at the other team's target. Whoever knocked down the opposing team's target would win.

Until he went to school, Rolihlahla had always worn the traditional clothes of his village: a blanket that was wrapped over one shoulder and pinned at the waist. At the Methodist school his mother had picked, however, the students dressed in the Western style, which meant wearing a shirt and trousers.

A shirt was found for him quickly enough, but trousers were more difficult, so Rolihlahla's father cut off a pair of his own trousers. They were roughly the right length, but much too big around the middle. However, with a rope tightened through the belt loops, they stayed firmly in place. Rolihlahla knew that the trousers did not really fit properly, but they were his father's, so he was proud to wear them.

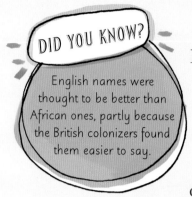

DID YOU KNOW?

English names were thought to be better than African ones, partly because the British colonizers found them easier to say.

One of the first things Rolihlahla's teacher, Miss Mdingane, did with the new students was to give them each an English name. At the time, being called by an English name was considered better than being called by an African one. Since the boys were about to receive a British education, the teachers believed each student should have an English name to match. The British didn't believe African culture was important. They thought British culture was superior.

From the moment Miss Mdingane gave him his English name, Rolihlahla would never be known as such to anyone outside his family again. His new English

---

what does "superior" mean?

Better than something. The British thought that their culture was superior to African culture.

name was the only one that would be used in school, and it was the name he would be known by from that day on.

Rolihlahla never learned why Miss Mdingane picked the name for him that she did. It was true that his new first name was the same as the last name of famous British naval hero Admiral Lord Nelson – but Rolihlahla didn't know if that was the reason he got it. All he knew for certain was that from that day on, he was known as Nelson.

Growing up fast

For the next two years, Nelson's life in Qunu was comfortable. He went to school, did chores around the kraal, and played with his friends.

One night, though, Nelson's father arrived home at an unexpected time, and the reason for this soon became clear. Gadla Henry was very ill. He was having trouble breathing, and could barely move. A few days later, he died.

Naturally, the death of his father was a significant moment in Nelson's life, but its importance went beyond losing a parent. Shortly afterwards, Chief Jongintaba Dalindyebo, whom Gadla Henry had long advised, became Nelson's guardian.

What is a guardian?

A person who is responsible for a child. The chief became Nelson's guardian and looked after him as one of his own.

Nelson's mother, Nosekeni Fanny, told her son that he was to be sent away to the king's home, known as the Great Place, in a village called Mqhekezweni (mu-KEH-zuh-when-ee). Nosekeni Fanny knew that by going away, the opportunities that would open up for Nelson would be far beyond what his mother could provide for him. Although she knew she would miss her son, his mother wanted the best for him.

Nelson adjusted quickly to his new life. He missed his mother, but, as he later wrote,

The king's compound in Mqhekezweni

This photograph of Chief Jongintaba Dalindyebo and his wife was taken in 1930, which was around the time Nelson came to live with them.

he found Mqhekezweni to be "a magical kingdom; everything was delightful… When I was not in school, I was a plowboy, a wagon guide, a shepherd. I rode horses and shot birds with slingshots and found boys to joust with."

Nelson did well in school and got along well with Jongintaba's son, Justice, and daughter, Nomafu. He ate what they ate and wore what they wore. Jongintaba and his wife treated Nelson fairly and with care. "Jongintaba was stern, but I never doubted his love," Nelson later said. The chief affectionately called Nelson by the name *Tatomkhulu*, meaning "grandpa", because Nelson so often looked very serious.

Not everything was easy, though. At home in Qunu, everyone simply used their

fingers to eat, but in Mqhekezweni forks and knives were the custom. Nelson was not used to them, and he was embarrassed about looking clumsy at meals. There were days when he ate less than he wanted for fear of looking foolish while fumbling with his utensils.

As time passed, the two anchors of Nelson's life became his education and his time in church. Until that point he had always considered the white European colonists as helpers to the black native people. Now, as a teenager studying history, geography, English, and the Bantu language Xhosa (KAW-suh), he began to see a different picture.

Visitors who came to the Great Place, especially a chief named Joyi, expressed the idea that the African people had been far better off on their own before the white men arrived. Nelson's emerging sense of

Christianity was
also troubled by the
limitations imposed
on black people. He
believed the church was
the ultimate moral guide
for how people should behave
towards one another – but if this
were true, he wondered, how could the church
support the oppression of the black people in
its community?

At 16 years old, Nelson had reached the
age at which the tradition of his tribe expected
him to become a man. As a man he would be
able to marry, own property, and participate
in tribal ceremonies. In order to achieve his
new status, Nelson, along with 24 other boys
his age, took part in several rituals to mark this
important occasion.

Nelson felt an understandable pride and
satisfaction at having reached this point in his
young life. His mood was sobered, though, by
the main speaker of the day, Chief Meligqili

DID YOU KNOW?

The Zion Christian
Church, founded in 1924
by native Africans, is
now the largest church
in South Africa.

(mel-leek-qwee-lee). Even years later, Nelson was to remember the chief's grim words.

"There sit our sons," said Chief Meligqili, "young, healthy, and handsome, the flower of the Xhosa tribe, the pride of our nation." However, Chief Meligqili was not hopeful about their futures. He declared that all black South Africans were "slaves in our own country". Therefore, the harsh truth was that the hopes and dreams of the boys would never be fulfilled. This was because the boys could not receive "the greatest gift of all, which is freedom and independence".

"We have promised them manhood... a promise that can never be fulfilled."

Chief Meligqili, as quoted in Nelson's autobiography, *Long Walk to Freedom*

Chapter

4

GETTING AN **education**

Nelson did not live at a time or in a place where he could expect to choose his own future. That decision was in the hands of Chief Jongintaba.

In the chief's eyes, the first thing Nelson needed was a more complete education. One day, if all went well, he expected that Nelson would become an advisor, much like Nelson's father had been before.

Nelson was sent to the Clarkebury Boarding Institute, in the town of Ngcobo. The school buildings were Western in style, rather than African.

Nelson was introduced to the headmaster, the Reverend Mr Harris, in his study. The reverend was warm and friendly towards Nelson, and they shook hands. Nelson was to remember later that it "was the first time I had ever shaken hands with a white man."

At his old school, Nelson was respected because the chief was his guardian – but at Clarkebury, nobody knew who Nelson's guardian was. And nobody cared. At Clarkebury, only Nelson's abilities and achievements would set him apart. Nelson knew that gaining respect from his teachers and fellow students would not be easy, because he had not yet excelled inside the classroom or outside on the playing fields.

In the beginning of his time at Clarkebury, if Nelson stood out at all, it was because he looked like he didn't belong. On the first day

of classes he had to wear boots for the first time, and his feet clattered so much on the polished wooden floors that some of his classmates laughed at him.

Three years later, in 1937, when Nelson was 19 years old, he moved on to Healdtown. Healdtown was a Methodist college in the town of Fort Beaufort, almost 325 km (200 miles) away.

At first, Nelson felt that it was almost like visiting another planet. Flushing toilets were new to him, as were pyjamas and toothpaste. (Before coming to Healdtown and learning what toothpaste was, Nelson whitened his teeth by rubbing ash on them.)

Nelson at 19 years old

The schedule there was rigorous. Breakfast was early, at 6:40 a.m., and it was nothing more than dry bread and hot sugar water. The morning was filled with four hours of classes. Lunch,

Samp was often mixed with beans.

which was at 12:45 p.m., usually featured sour milk and beans, and dried corn kernels, called samp. Classes continued for another four hours, followed by a break for exercise and dinner. An evening of homework ended with lights out at 9:30 p.m.

At Healdtown, Nelson participated in school sports for the first time. He took up cross-country running and boxing, both of which took discipline and helped him to fit in with the other students. At first, he was not especially good at either, but through practice – and by gaining a bit more muscle – he soon improved.

As for his classroom education, Nelson was not just gaining academic knowledge.

DID YOU KNOW?

While attending Fort Hare, Nelson took ballroom dancing classes.

He was also gaining a better understanding of the limitations a black man faced in the white man's world. This growing awareness continued to build as he moved on to the University College of Fort Hare, in the town of Alice, in 1939. There, as at his other schools, he remembered being taught that he should respect the political authorities and be thankful for the educational opportunities given to him by the church and by the government.

As his thinking grew more sophisticated, though, it was difficult for Nelson to make all these ideas fit nicely together. On the one hand, he was being taught to use logic to solve problems and work out situations. On the other hand, he was also being told to accept certain social and political boundaries that were ingrained in society. And these, he was well aware, were not really logical at all.

Being clear about his ideas helped Nelson to develop a new sense of independence. In his second year at Fort Hare he was elected to the Student Representative Council. When the university administration refused to grant the council some of the authority the council believed it should have, Nelson resigned in protest. He had the power to do that – but the university had power, too. The principal chose to send him home early for what he called insubordination.

What is insubordination?

Insubordination means to disobey an order from a higher authority. The headmaster judged that Nelson was insubordinate when he resigned from the student council.

Chief Jongintaba was surprised and displeased to see Nelson come home before his term at Fort Hare was over. He made it clear to Nelson that he, the chief, was in charge of Nelson's life. The boy should simply do as he was told. To make this point even clearer, the chief soon informed Nelson that he had chosen a wife for him to marry.

Now it was Nelson's turn to be surprised. He didn't know if arranging a marriage was the chief's way of reminding him who was the boss in their relationship, or whether the chief genuinely thought this young woman was the perfect partner for Nelson. Either way, he

ARRANGED MARRIAGE

It was common in many societies (and still is in some cultures today) for parents or guardians to arrange the marriages of their children. The reasons behind the matchmaking were often quite practical. Money was a common factor because the fortunes of two families would be joined together by the union. Or it might be that the two sets of parents simply liked the idea of their families becoming related through marriage.

knew better than to argue because, as his
guardian, the chief had the traditional right
to arrange such a marriage. Yet that didn't mean
Nelson would meekly accept his decision. Nelson
was stubborn, just as his father had been, but he
knew he could not refuse the arranged marriage
and continue to live under the chief's roof. His
only alternative was to run away.

And so, in 1941, at the age of 22, he did.

Chapter **5**

Fighting FOR A cause

When Nelson decided to run away, there was no question about where he would go. His destination was Johannesburg.

In Johannesburg, the largest city in South Africa, Nelson believed he might be able to improve his social status and achieve his goals. He was also very excited about seeing a place he had heard so much about. In his mind the city had almost a mythical status.

The city of Johannesburg as it looked in the 1940s

36

Johannesburg was not simply a larger version of a town. He had been told stories of "buildings so tall you could not see the tops, of crowds of people speaking languages you had never heard of…" What should he do once he got to Johannesburg? Nelson wasn't sure. He hadn't done much planning in advance, so it took him some time to settle in. He worked as a night watchman in a mine and as an estate agent while he finished

his university degree with courses he completed through the post.

For all the time that he was growing up, Nelson had always imagined himself returning home to Qunu at some point to take up a career. In 1943, he enrolled at law school because it seemed like the logical next step,

"Johannesburg had always been **depicted** as a **city of dreams**, a place where one could **transform oneself** from a **poor peasant** to a **wealthy sophisticate...**"

Nelson Mandela,
Long Walk to Freedom

but he did not really apply himself to his courses. And, in the end, he did not meet the requirements for graduation.

Nelson had only been in Johannesburg for a short time when he started to focus more on political activism. He wanted to change things in the government. The central problem facing black people in South Africa was the crushing oppression they met at every turn. Black people were kept down and not allowed the same opportunities or freedoms that were allowed to others. After the British created the Union of South Africa in 1910, new laws were designed and enforced to keep black people from pursuing any number of careers.

FORGIVE AND FORGET

Towards the end of 1941, Nelson's guardian, Chief Jongintaba, visited Johannesburg and met Nelson, forgiving him for running away. Jongintaba died only a few months later.

It didn't matter how clever they were or how hard they worked. They were trapped in a web of regulations that kept progress out of reach. Nelson clearly saw the widespread injustice in this system, and he was determined to do something about it and help his people.

To make sure his efforts were as effective as possible, he joined the African National Congress (ANC). The ANC was an organization trying to improve the conditions for black South Africans. Its protests, though, were largely very

NEW LAWS

In 1911, the Mines and Works Act was passed. It meant that black South Africans worked in low-paying jobs. The more skilled, higher-paying jobs, such as surveying, were reserved for whites. Two years later, the Natives Land Act severely limited where black people could own land. Even when they were allowed to own it, this land had little value. It was always set deep in the countryside, far from the cities. Could black people hope for change through the political process? Not really. The Native Representation Act of 1936 meant that only high-class black people could vote – so most couldn't – and they could only vote for white candidates.

The ANC had its roots in the South African Native National Congress. Some of its members are shown here in 1914.

polite efforts. Petitions would be circulated and signed by black people. These petitions were then submitted to the white authorities, who would either ignore them or bury them in administrative red tape.

The aim of Nelson and his friends was to transform the ANC from a small group

what does "red tape" mean? Red tape is lots of unnecessary paperwork demanded by governments or big businesses. The South African authorities used red tape as a way of avoiding dealing with the petitions.

of intellectual activists into a much larger organization. It would have a mass membership of black people from all over the country. Educated or not, these people had never been given the chance to speak up. They had suffered largely in silence. Maybe now their voices would be heard.

As a first step, Nelson and some others created the African National Congress Youth League in 1944. They intended to change things politically, to make life better for black people. They wanted more rights relating to voting and land ownership. They called for free education for all children regardless of their skin colour.

Nelson was passionate about these issues, but he still had a personal life. One of his friends in the ANC, Walter Sisulu, had a cousin called Evelyn, who was a nurse.

Walter Sisulu

Here's Nelson.

This is Evelyn.

Nelson and Evelyn, as bridesmaid, were guests at
Walter Sisulu's wedding.

She and Nelson soon started dating, and a few
months later, they were married. For now the
pieces of Nelson's life had fallen into place.
Yet even though those pieces seemed to fit
together well, it was not clear for how long they
would continue to do so.

Revolutionary thoughts

Nelson had opposed many South African laws because they kept black people from freely improving their lives.

These prohibitions, bad as they were, soon became much worse. In 1948, the new all-white Afrikaner National Party took control of the government. Soon after that, South Africa made into law the policy of apartheid.

Apartheid formally separated black people from white people in many ways. It kept people apart politically, socially, and economically on the basis of their race. Black people would now have to live in separate areas from whites. Marriages between them were banned. Black South Africans were also separated from one another by their tribal backgrounds.

PROTESTS AGAINST APARTHEID

At first, there was little response from other countries to South Africa's new policy of apartheid. However, some people did form groups to protest. Unfortunately, although these protests received some attention, the laws remained in force.

People protesting against racial discrimination in London, England

This was a political strategy, or plan. If tribes were kept apart, they were unlikely ever to come together to threaten the existing authority.

The government did not even pretend that these changes were in any way for the benefit or the good of black people. It was cold and ruthless in its mission to put black people in their place and keep them there. No change, no new regulation, that would achieve this was too outrageous to propose.

Although the white people of South Africa were comfortable with apartheid because of their sense of superiority, there was another

LAND REFORMS

A few years later, in the 1950s, further steps were taken to strengthen white control. Black people were often forcibly removed from the parts of the countryside where they had lived for generations. The land they left behind was then sold to white farmers at artificially low prices. As white people became increasingly wealthier than black people, whites gained even more control of the country.

reason they wanted
these new laws in place.
That reason was fear.
For all of the power they
held over black South
Africans, white people
were still a minority when it
came to actual numbers. This
knowledge made them nervous. To overcome
this fear, they tried to build up as much support
from the legal system as they could get.

As things turned out, the new policies
triggered huge outrage. The black activists
living in South Africa reacted to apartheid
with renewed energy.

In 1949, the ANC pushed hard to become
a much bigger organization. No longer would
its members be content to raise their hands
politely when objecting to government policies.
Previously, ANC members had tried to keep
their protests within legal bounds – an approach
that had clearly not brought them much success.
Their new strategy would call for more action.

TREASON TRIAL

Nelson Mandela and the other activists were gathered up in raids around the country and arrested for their allegedly treasonous activities. Eventually all of the accused were set free.

They would focus on passive resistance. This meant that their protests would not use violence. There were risks in taking even non-violent actions, but Nelson and his colleagues were willing to accept those risks.

In the next few years, Nelson was repeatedly arrested for joining in protests around the country. In 1952, he was one of the leaders of the ANC's Campaign for the Defiance of Unjust Laws. Nelson was committed to protesting against apartheid whatever the price he might personally have to pay. He worked with the ANC and other organizations to write the Freedom Charter, which set out rules for a fairer society. This led, in 1956–1961, to Nelson and 155 activists being unsuccessfully prosecuted for treason.

In 1952, Nelson founded a law firm with Oliver Tambo, a former friend from his school days. Their aim was not to

Oliver Tambo

make money, although some payment would certainly have been welcome since neither of them had independent sources of income. Their main purpose was to provide free or low-cost legal representation to black people in need.

All of this activity, however, came at a price for Nelson's family. His fight against injustice for black South Africans consumed him. Nelson remembered later that it was during this period that his wife, Evelyn, told him that their "elder son, Thembi, then five,

had asked her, 'Where does Daddy live?' I had been returning home late at night, long after he had gone to sleep, and departing early in the morning before he woke."

Evelyn harboured resentments of her own. Certainly, she had married Nelson for love, but her dreams differed from his. Evelyn had expected that his life would be a normal one devoted to his family and a regular job. Nelson wrote that she could not live with him being devoted to something apart from herself and their family. The harder Nelson worked, the more their relationship suffered. They managed to stay together for a few more years, but finally divorced in 1958.

7

Raising the stakes

Nelson had been committed to non-violent protest. His hope was that the government would see the error of its prejudiced ways.

However, there was a problem. This hope was based on the idea that the government would actually *want* to be shown the error of its prejudiced ways. The South African government wasn't actually interested in seeing this at all. Its politicians knew their laws were prejudiced against black South Africans. They knew that these laws would oppress, or keep down, black people and keep them serving the needs of white people. The truth was, they liked things that way.

---

what does "prejudice" mean?

Prejudice is having unfair feelings against certain people. The government was prejudiced against black South Africans.

Nelson and his comrades began to feel that non-violent actions were not the answer. In 1960, a peaceful protest ended in the police shooting dead many protesters. It became known as the Sharpeville Massacre. This terrible event helped confirm to Nelson and his fellow activists that more violent steps were now necessary.

The activists knew that using violence would be dangerous, and they were afraid for their own

SHARPEVILLE MASSACRE

On 21 March 1960, a crowd of several thousand protesters went to the local police station at Sharpeville in the Transvaal. Although the crowd was unarmed, police officers opened fire. They continued to shoot even as the crowd fled in fear. Sixty-nine people were killed and more than 400 were wounded, including women and children. Even under the laws of apartheid, the massacre created a crisis for the government.

Black protesters being fired at by police

safety. However, as Nelson later wrote, "The brave man is not he who does not feel afraid, but he who conquers that fear."

It was just a few years earlier that Nelson had met Nomzamo Winnie Madikizela. She was the first black female social worker ever trained in South Africa and an active member of the ANC. As Nelson later wrote, "I cannot say for certain if there is such a thing as love at first sight, but I do know that the moment I first glimpsed Winnie Nomzamo, I knew that I wanted to have her as my wife."

Unlike Nelson's first wife, Evelyn, Winnie was well aware of Nelson's priorities. His law practice was not going well, but he was unwilling to sacrifice any of the time he was devoting to the ANC. He told Winnie that they would very likely have to live on her small salary as a social worker. Winnie understood and was prepared to do this.

Eventually, after years of peaceful protests, and no changes by the government, Nelson

Nelson married Winnie on 14 June 1958. They later had two children together.

saw violent protest as the only way to get the white minority to listen. In 1961, new tactics began, including planting bombs in places like electrical plants or transport facilities. Nelson did not pretend that these actions were not violent. However, targets were chosen to avoid loss of life as much as possible.

During this time, warrants were issued for Nelson's arrest. His many friends and supporters helped to keep him hidden. He also escaped capture by sometimes travelling in disguise. At one point he drove around the country giving speeches while pretending to be a chauffeur.

However, Nelson's luck finally ran out. He was captured in August 1962 and accused

False travel documents used by Nelson in 1962

of various crimes against the state. At his trial he did not really defend himself. (He actually agreed that he was guilty of the charges.) Instead, he concentrated on promoting the ANC cause. His actions were reluctant ones, he insisted. Desperate times, he argued, called for desperate actions.

The court did not agree. Nelson was sentenced to five years in prison. However, the next year he was found to be connected to other illegal activities against the government. The charges were serious. Once more he was accused of sabotage. A second trial took place between October 1963 and June 1964.

Outside the court, a large crowd gathered to protest. Towards the end of the trial, Nelson made an impassioned speech. His words rang out, not only in the courtroom, but also later throughout the country and around the world.

"During my lifetime," he stated, "I have dedicated myself to this struggle of the African people. I have fought against white domination, and I have fought against black domination. I have cherished the ideal of a democratic and free society in which all persons live together in harmony and with equal opportunities. It is an ideal which I

---

what does "sabotage" mean?

To destroy or damage a plan or property. The revolutionaries sabotaged power plants to stop them from working.

hope to live for and to achieve. But if need be, it is an ideal for which I am prepared to die."

When the verdict was announced, Nelson and the others were found guilty. They were sentenced to life imprisonment. It was a scary moment. If the sentences were carried out, only death would set them free.

Chapter 8

Life behind bars

Robben Island lies little more than 6.5 km (4 miles) off the lower west coast of South Africa.

The island had long been used as a place for people who were classed as "undesirables" – people who were not wanted. It had once been a colony for people who suffered from the disease of leprosy. Usually, though, Robben Island served as a jail for political prisoners and convicted criminals. And that was its purpose when Nelson was sent there in 1964.

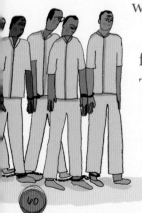

Nelson and six fellow prisoners faced a difficult journey to the island. They were taken away in the middle of the night, under heavy police guard. They soon arrived at a small military airport and boarded

This is how the entrance to the Robben Island prison looks today. It is no longer used to keep prisoners, and is now a UNESCO World Heritage site that is open to visitors.

an old plane. The prisoners were frightened – some had never flown before.

Upon arriving on the island, Nelson and the other prisoners were met by armed guards. Nelson remembered the chill winter wind blowing through their thin prison uniforms.

Nelson was initially classified as the lowest grade of prisoner – Class D. This meant that he was allowed one visit and one letter every six months. At first, Nelson was housed with several other prisoners, but in later years, he lived alone in a small, damp concrete cell. When Nelson lay down, he could feel one wall at his feet while the other end grazed the top of his head. The cell had no mattress or bed – only a flat straw mat to sleep on. As for the food, Nelson later recorded his opinion. He recalled that the authorities liked to say that prisoners received a balanced diet. Nelson agreed that it was balanced – a balance between tasteless and uneatable.

Every morning, Nelson, along with the other prisoners, waited while a load of stones

This was Nelson Mandela's prison cell on Robben Island.

was dumped on the ground outside. Each stone was about as big as a volleyball. The prisoners' job was to crush the stones into gravel using a hammer.

Nine months later, Nelson began working at a limestone quarry. There, he extracted limestone from layers of rock

with a pick and shovel. The commander in charge assured the prisoners that this kind of heavy labour would last for six months at most. That turned out to be a lie. The prisoners worked at the quarry for much longer than six months – they worked there for 13 years.

Physical hardships were not the only worries. A prisoner's mental health was always vulnerable. No matter how strong-willed the prisoners were, the prison environment was designed to break them. If the men had been isolated, or kept alone, they might not have been able to survive. Fortunately, the authorities kept the prisoners together, and being together, they could draw on mutual support.

"We supported each other and gained strength from each other. Whatever we knew, whatever we learned, we shared..."

From Nelson's autobiography, *Long Walk to Freedom*

Even though he was in prison, Nelson continued to work hard to support people. He offered guidance and leadership to many of his fellow inmates, representing them in grievances with prison authorities. Gradually, his living conditions improved. In the 1970s, he was allowed more visitors and greater freedom to correspond by mail.

Secondary school students in Soweto, South Africa, protesting for a better education in 1976

Meanwhile, the force of apartheid continued to oppress black South Africans. On 16 June 1976, between 10,000 and 20,000 children marched in protest in the township of Soweto. The crowd was peaceful and unarmed, but the police became alarmed and eventually began shooting at them. Twenty-three people died in that first response. More protests followed, leading to further deaths.

With Nelson and other leaders in prison, and the ANC barred from the country and in exile, other people took the lead. In the late 1960s, another group in South Africa, the Black People's Convention, arose to challenge the institution of apartheid. One of its leaders was Steve Biko, who was threatened several times by the authorities. Finally arrested in 1977, he was severely beaten while in custody. He died from this attack. His death inspired people to continue to protest even more strongly against apartheid.

Such incidents brought the problems in South Africa to people's attention all around the world. Boycotts of South African companies were organized. This meant that people withdrew from

STEVE BIKO

Steve Biko was born in 1946. He was a member of the Xhosa people in the Eastern Cape, a province of South Africa. While growing up, Steve planned to study law, but he changed his mind and decided to study medicine at the University of Natal. However, law again became his focus when he struggled against unjust laws in the fight against apartheid.

trading with South Africa. Many
foreign leaders protested against the
prejudicial system that had been in place
for decades. In 1980, the United Nations
Security Council called for Nelson's release.
The request was ignored.

Through it all, Nelson's spirits remained
strong. "I never seriously considered the
possibility that I would not emerge from prison
one day," he wrote later. "I never thought that a
life sentence truly meant life and that I would die
behind bars. Perhaps I was denying this prospect
because it was too unpleasant to contemplate."

Chapter

9

Freedom

Although some changes to apartheid took place in the 1980s, the government under President P.W. Botha continued to oppress black people.

Botha, known as "The Great Crocodile", had the reputation of being a stubborn man. In a major speech given in 1985, Botha refused to change the apartheid system. He

was not going to be the one to change a policy and way of life that had been in place for so many years. He also refused to release Nelson Mandela from prison, despite requests from many international figures and organizations.

P.W. Botha

Both these decisions sparked strong reactions from the international community. Many countries were now punishing South Africa for its policies by refusing to invest in South African companies. Many international corporations withdrew support as well. The rest of the world was waking up and paying attention to what was happening in South Africa.

Only when a new president, F.W. de Klerk, was elected in 1989, however, did dramatic changes occur. Originally viewed as simply the latest in a long line of apartheid-supporting leaders, de Klerk surprised many onlookers with a more understanding outlook. De Klerk was well aware that the tensions between black and white South Africans were growing. The country might soon erupt into a racial civil war. If that happened, South Africa would be torn apart.

To lessen these tensions, the de Klerk government began allowing anti-apartheid groups to meet. Most importantly, he ordered the release of prisoners who had been convicted for their anti-apartheid activities. Among them was Nelson Mandela.

During the 27 years Nelson had spent in prison, the world had changed in many ways. Important civil rights acts had been passed in the United States. People had landed on the Moon. An American president had been forced to resign in disgrace. The Soviet Union had fallen apart. Nations that had belonged to the Soviet Union had once again become independent countries.

Also, while in prison, Nelson had suffered two terrible losses. In 1968, his mother died. A year later,

In Soweto, an overjoyed boy holds up a newspaper announcing Nelson's release from prison. It made headline news around the world.

his eldest son, Thembi, died in a car accident. Nelson was not allowed to attend the funerals.

Nelson's release in February 1990 ushered in a new era in South African life. He had already met President de Klerk during the last months of his imprisonment, which helped to ensure that de Klerk made good his promise to dismantle some apartheid restrictions.

One of the first places Nelson visited as a free man was Soweto, the scene of so much violence and unhappiness. There, 120,000 people gathered to hear him speak. Nelson spoke plainly. Injustice, he insisted, was no excuse for unacceptable behaviour.

As he emerged from prison, with Winnie by his
side, Nelson raised his fist in the traditional ANC
salute. The act was met with a great roar from
the waiting crowd.

Nelson said that he had heard of criminals pretending to be political activists, preying on innocent people and setting alight vehicles. These criminals had no place in the struggle against apartheid. Violence was not the answer – they must make progress peacefully.

Within a few months Nelson was hard at work within the ANC to build on the changes that President de Klerk had started to set up. He also travelled abroad, meeting many foreign leaders, including Pope John Paul II, Prime Minister Margaret Thatcher of the United Kingdom, and presidents George H.W. Bush of the United States, Fidel Castro of Cuba, and François Mitterrand of France.

Several conferences that sought to move things
forward were then held within South Africa, but
it was unclear at first what the outcome might be.
Some South Africans wanted things to continue
the way they were. Others wanted South Africa
to be broken up into more than one country as a
way to ensure that black people would have their
proper rights.

Several uncertain years passed before the
government took on a new shape, one that
Nelson and the ANC had worked to create and
could support. After more than three centuries

DID YOU KNOW?

In 1994, Nelson's autobiography, *Long Walk to Freedom*, much of which was written in prison, was published.

of rule, the white minority was admitting defeat and turning over power to the black majority. In April 1994, new elections were held, and the ANC swept into power. Members of the new National Assembly then formally elected Nelson as the country's first black president. It was a truly historic moment, but as Nelson said, it did not represent the end of his quest. "We have not taken the final step of our journey," he said, "but the first step on a longer and even more difficult road."

"... to be free is not merely to cast off one's chains, but to live in a way that respects and enhances the freedom of others."

Nelson Mandela, from his autobiography, *Long Walk to Freedom*

Chapter 10

Revolutionary ideals

The new president of South Africa was 77 years old when he took office. The years Nelson had spent in prison had taken a physical toll.

Nelson had suffered from both tuberculosis and cancer before assuming the presidency. Still, he felt full of new energy at the idea of finally getting rid of apartheid, which had plagued his country for so long. Nelson made a powerful speech when he was sworn in as president: "The time for the healing of wounds has come. The moment to bridge the chasms that divided us has come. The time to build is upon us. We have, at last, achieved our political emancipation." Nelson meant by this that his people had achieved political freedom.

In a way, Nelson's goal was simple. He wanted to make sure that black people and white people were treated equally. However, achieving this goal would not be simple at all. It was daunting. Nelson did not want to swap one kind of oppression for another, and he didn't want to use force to bluntly and perhaps violently achieve the changes he wanted. He knew certain changes required patience and a delicate touch. "In nation building," he wrote, "you sometimes need a bulldozer, and sometimes a feather duster."

He was also not seeking revenge. The past was filled with outrages and injustices, but he couldn't change the past – although if there were injustices that could be addressed and corrected he certainly wanted to do so. He knew that instituting, or making into law, a new round of punishments would only make people feel bitter on both sides.

What President Mandela hoped and worked for was a peaceful transition, or change, to a new South African reality. He didn't want to punish white people for their past behaviour. At the same time he made it clear that this behaviour would no longer be tolerated.

Nelson stands to attention as the South African national anthem is played during his presidential inauguration at the Union Building in Pretoria, South Africa, on 10 May 1994.

A supporter waves an ANC flag during Nelson Mandela's presidential inauguration.

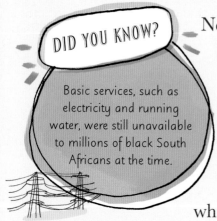

DID YOU KNOW?

Basic services, such as electricity and running water, were still unavailable to millions of black South Africans at the time.

Nelson kept a careful balance between compromise and change. He wanted to ensure that basic human needs of housing and health care were met for everyone, black and white alike. The policies governing land ownership, for example, which had excluded black people for so long, needed a complete overhaul.

All these changes represented a huge upheaval. Nelson, however, was determined to make these changes while keeping racial harmony between the people. One of Nelson's largest concerns, or worries, was South Africa's economic health. The country would be in big trouble if the white population became so afraid or disenchanted that they chose to leave South Africa, taking their skills and resources with them.

What is disenchanted?

Disenchanted means no longer to be in favour of something. Nelson was worried that the white people in South Africa might become disenchanted with the new regime.

"At a time when some of the **most vibrant economies** in the world have been **buffeted by storms,** we have performed relatively well."

Nelson Mandela, from his New Year's message as president, 31 December 1997

In 1996, two years after becoming president, Nelson signed into law a new constitution. It was a historic moment. Freedom of expression would now be available to anyone and everyone regardless of their political leanings. This meant that people were free to speak out about their beliefs. These changes reflected Nelson's idea that a government could not only survive, but actually improve, by listening to criticism that might come its way.

Sometimes, Nelson found that a symbol of progress could be as powerful and influential as any new law. In 1995, South Africa hosted the

CONSTITUTION

A constitution is a set of laws that governs an organization or country. The new South African constitution ensured the government was ruled by the majority, in which all people of all colours and religions were eligible to vote. Those opposing the government would no longer be able to be arrested and imprisoned simply for their beliefs.

Nelson meeting the South African national rugby team, the Springboks, at the Rugby World Cup in May 1995.

Rugby World Cup. This was a very important step forward for South Africa. Under the rules of apartheid, black people had not been able to play for the national team, the Springboks. Apartheid might now have been abolished, but bad feeling towards the Springboks remained because the team was still mostly made up of white people. The Springboks went on to win the cup. Nelson publicly showed his support for the Springboks, and he encouraged all black citizens to follow his example.

Nelson's interest extended far beyond the South African borders. Whether he wanted it or not, Nelson had become a symbol of Africa as a whole. He used that position to promote more improvements. In a speech helping to launch the "Kick Polio Out of Africa" campaign (which used a football as its symbol), he said, "Africa is renowned for its beauty, its rich natural heritage, and huge resources – but equally, the image of its suffering children haunts the conscience of our continent and the world."

"KICK POLIO OUT OF AFRICA"

Polio is a disease that often leads to loss of movement. It continued to affect people in Africa, especially children, long after it had been removed from most other parts of the world. The campaign against polio encouraged the use of vaccination as a way of getting rid of the disease.

President Nelson Mandela chats with Deputy President Thabo Mbeki as he attends his last cabinet meeting, on 9 June 1999.

Nelson Mandela's whole term as president was dominated by moving on from the oppressive regime of the past, which had kept black people down for so long. Now having reached his eighties, Nelson recognized that it was time to step back from daily political responsibilities. He had long maintained that he would serve only one term – and as so many people already knew about Nelson, he was a man of his word.

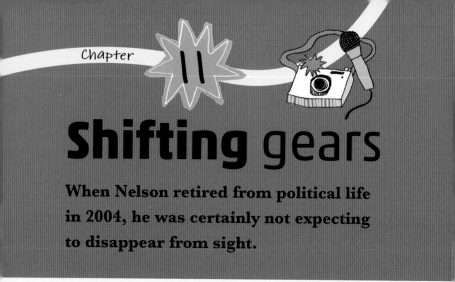

Chapter 11

Shifting gears

When Nelson retired from political life in 2004, he was certainly not expecting to disappear from sight.

He had become much more than a high-ranking government figure in South Africa. Nelson was now an international celebrity, and he hoped to use his fame and influence to further worthy causes. Among the organizations he helped to establish was the Nelson Mandela Foundation. Its mission was to help make a just and free society that treated people with fairness, wherever they came from.

Nelson Mandela and singer and activist Bob Geldof speaking at the launch of the Make Poverty History campaign rally in London, England, in 2005.

MAKE POVERTY **HISTORY**

There was still much Nelson hoped to achieve. He was committed to fighting for human rights around the world. He also fought to raise awareness of the AIDS epidemic. The cumulative effects of AIDS had been devastating. More than 30 million people had been infected around the world. Nelson's son Makhatho died of AIDS in 2005, at the age of 55. Nelson described AIDS as "one of the greatest threats humankind has faced".

WHAT IS AIDS?

AIDS is an infection that attacks the human body's immune system (which helps keep the body free from infection). It is caused by the virus HIV. From the 1980s, AIDS spread rapidly all over the world. Its effects have been particularly deadly in Africa. Nelson dedicated himself to promoting the cause of making life-saving drugs more widely available.

Nelson Mandela with AIDS activist Zackie Achmat

Nelson celebrated his 90th birthday surrounded by his grandchildren on 18 July 2008.

Nelson also wanted to spend more time with his family. He could not replace the time he had lost with his children and grandchildren because of prison and his career, but he could at least see them more often now that the daily responsibilities of political life had been removed.

His personal life had also taken another turn. After his divorce from Winnie, he had come to know Graça Machel, a former education minister in Mozambique. Her husband, Samora Machel, the president of Mozambique, had died in a plane crash in 1986.

Graça was 27 years younger than Nelson, and at first they simply became good friends. While Graça continued her humanitarian work on behalf of refugees, her friendship with Nelson deepened as they spent more and more time together. They were finally married in 1998, just before Mandela's term as president ended.

GRAÇA MACHEL

Graça Machel was born in 1945 and grew up in the southern African country of Mozambique. She attended the University of Lisbon in Portugal, where she first took an interest in issues of independence. When Mozambique declared its independence from Portugal in 1975, she became its first Minister for Education and Culture.

Queen Sofía of Spain talks to Nelson Mandela at a pre-wedding royal dinner in Madrid in 2004.

Nelson Mandela sits with US president George W. Bush in the White House's Oval Office in May 2005.

British prime minister Gordon Brown greets Nelson Mandela at Downing Street, London, in August 2007.

Although he lacked the energy of earlier years, Nelson still travelled widely and hosted leaders who came to visit him. When speaking at the birthday celebration of his friend Walter Sisulu in 2002, he said, "What counts in life is not the mere fact that we have lived."

Nelson continued to face a number of health issues. He had survived several bouts of cancer by the time he decided to retire formally from public life in 2004. He then returned to his home in the village of Qunu where he had lived as a boy so many years before.

"It is **what difference** we **have made** to the lives of others that will determine the **significance** of **the life** we lead."

From a speech by Nelson during the 90th birthday celebrations of his friend Walter Sisulu in 2002

But he had not finished yet. On his birthday, 18 July, in 2007, Nelson and Graça announced the creation of a new organization, the Elders. Its members were retired political and religious leaders, who viewed themselves as independent world leaders working together for peace and human rights. Membership of the Elders included Kofi Annan, former United Nations Secretary General; Jimmy Carter, former United States president; and Li Zhaoxing, former Foreign Minister of the People's Republic of China. The group's small size reflected Nelson's preference for one-on-one meetings over large organized gatherings. In the years since, they have worked to promote women's equality and dealt with humanitarian crises such as famine.

Nelson's reputation as a worldwide champion of democracy and social justice was further underscored in 2009. On his birthday that year, the United Nations declared 18 July to be known forever as Nelson Mandela International Day in honour of his contributions to peace and human rights. In keeping with Nelson's spirit, the day was not meant to be a holiday, but a day devoted to the idea of making the world a better place for everyone who lives in it.

A year later, in 2010, Nelson made his final public appearance at the end of the football World Cup tournament in South Africa. Three years after that, on 5 December 2013, at the age of 95, Nelson died.

South African fans show their support for Nelson at the opening ceremony ahead of the 2010 FIFA World Cup in South Africa.

Nelson and his wife, Graça, wave to the crowd before the 2010 World Cup final between the Netherlands and Spain on 11 July.

12

Remembered

Nelson's death itself was not a surprise to his family. They had gathered at his bedside knowing the end was near.

Nelson Mandela had lived through the end of World War I, the entirety of World War II, the invention of frozen foods, television, and mobile phones. Explorers in his youth were still circling the globe in ships – now, astronauts orbited the Earth from space.

Perhaps most of all, Nelson had witnessed the peaceful growth of incredible political and social change in South Africa. The country was hardly perfect. It had some of the same shortcomings as other countries, such as the inequality between rich and poor. But South Africa had fundamentally transformed from the rigid, racially based society of the early 1900s, and Nelson had led the charge for that change for more than 70 years.

Jacob Zuma

Upon the news of Nelson's death, Jacob Zuma, the president of South Africa, released a statement. He declared that whether in South Africa or somewhere else in the world, people should continue to follow Nelson's vision of a way of life in which everyone treated one another with respect and fairness: "Let us reaffirm his vision of a society in which none is exploited, oppressed, or dispossessed by another."

CHANGES IN SOUTH AFRICA

By the time of Nelson's death, South Africa was a vibrant part of the international community. This was only possible because of the changes that had come to South Africa. Black people now had the same political rights as white people, which had enormous social, economic, and cultural consequences.

"When a man has done what he considers to be his duty to his country and his people, he can rest in peace."

Nelson Mandela, speaking after suffering from an infection in his nineties

Tributes quickly poured in from all over the world. "Nelson Mandela's shining example and his political legacy of non-violence and the condemnation of all forms of racism will continue to inspire people around the world for many years to come", said German chancellor Angela Merkel. Israeli prime minister Benjamin Netanyahu noted, "He was the father of his people, a man of vision, a freedom fighter who rejected violence." American television talk show host Oprah Winfrey remembered, "Being in his presence was like sitting with grace and majesty at the same time."

Today in South Africa, Nelson Mandela is often called the "Father of the Nation". Throughout his life he was certainly happy to accept a compliment, but he would have been the first to declare that he was far from perfect. He made mistakes like everyone else – but to the world, perhaps his flaws had faded into the background while his better qualities had stepped to the front.

A sea of flowers lies at the road's edge as crowds gather to pay their respects at Nelson Mandela's Johannesburg home. This was only a few days after the former leader's death was announced. Although Mandela had been ill for some time, his death still sparked an outpouring of grief and dismay.

The British leader Winston Churchill, upon hearing one of his opponents described as a modest man, immediately replied that the man had a lot to be modest about. Nelson's supporters and opponents alike described him as a stubborn man. However, considering the oppression and difficulties he had confronted in his lifetime, truly he had much to be stubborn about.

Certainly, Nelson could never have survived so many obstacles without a fierce stubbornness to help him through hard times. His long life had been marked with hurdles: the early death of his father, his interrupted education, his time as a hunted activist, and,

The largest statue of Nelson Mandela in the world is 8 m (26 ft) high. It stands on Naval Hill in Bloemfontein, the city of roses, in South Africa.

most of all, his 27 years in prison, would have broken a lesser man.

Yet this same stubbornness, fed by his faith in the righteousness of his ideals, had not led to anger or resentment. No one would have faulted Nelson for seeking revenge against those who had unjustly harmed him. But Nelson stubbornly resisted taking that path as well. Given what he had endured, he was also the most forgiving of men.

DID YOU KNOW?

Nelson was often called "Madiba" by close friends and family. It was a tribal name bestowed as a sign of great respect.

MADIBA SHIRT

The Madiba shirt, made popular by Nelson, is made of silk and usually has a bold and colourful print. The shirt was named after Nelson's nickname. He wore them often, to social gatherings and more formal business or political meetings. People still wear the Madiba shirt today.

He wrote, "No one is born hating another person because of the colour of his skin, or his background, or his religion. People must learn to hate, and if they can learn to hate, they can be taught to love, for love comes more naturally to the human heart than its opposite."

Nelson Mandela believed that people, whatever their faults, are capable of doing better. Nelson, and the people that he guided, brought freedom and fairness to South Africa and set an example of peace that has inspired others all over the world.

Nelson's
family tree

First
wife

Evelyn Ntoko Mase
1922–2004

Son

Madiba
Thembekile
Mandela
1945–1969

Makaziwe
Mandela
1948–1948
(aged nine months)

Daughter

Magkatho
Lewanika
Mandela
1950–2005

Son

Pumla
Makaziwe
Mandela
1954–

Daughter

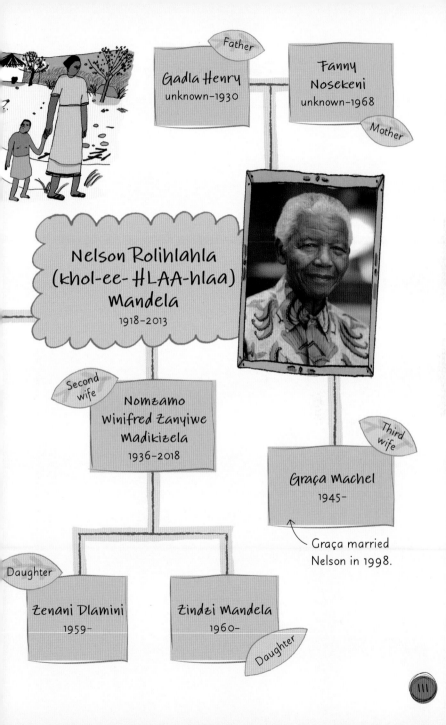

Father
Gadla Henry
unknown–1930

Fanny
Nosekeni
unknown–1968
Mother

Nelson Rolihlahla
(khol-ee-HLAA-hlaa)
Mandela
1918–2013

Second
wife
Nomzamo
Winifred Zanyiwe
Madikizela
1936–2018

Third
wife
Graça Machel
1945–

↑
Graça married
Nelson in 1998.

Daughter
Zenani Dlamini
1959–

Zindzi Mandela
1960–
Daughter

111

Timeline

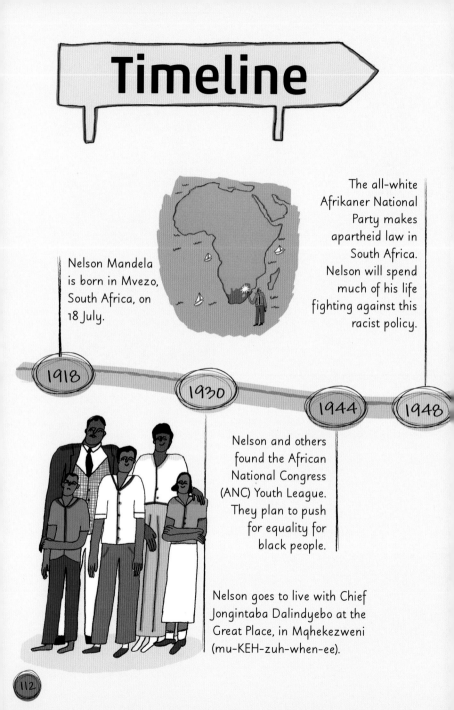

Nelson Mandela is born in Mvezo, South Africa, on 18 July.

The all-white Afrikaner National Party makes apartheid law in South Africa. Nelson will spend much of his life fighting against this racist policy.

1918

1930

1944

1948

Nelson and others found the African National Congress (ANC) Youth League. They plan to push for equality for black people.

Nelson goes to live with Chief Jongintaba Dalindyebo at the Great Place, in Mqhekezweni (mu-KEH-zuh-when-ee).

Nelson marries Winnie Madikizela on 14 June.

Nelson is one of the leaders of the ANC's Campaign for the Defiance of Unjust Laws.

On 21 March, in the township of Sharpeville, police open fire on a crowd of unarmed protesters, killing 69 people. It became known as the Sharpeville Massacre.

1952

1958

1960

1962

Nelson starts a law firm with his school friend, Oliver Tambo, to give free or low-cost legal services to black people in need.

Nelson is arrested and accused of crimes against the state. He is sentenced to five years in prison.

113

Nelson is tried for more crimes against the government. He is sentenced to life imprisonment and is sent to Robben Island.

Nelson turns 70 in prison. A concert in the UK celebrates his birthday, and 200 million people around the world tune in to watch it on television.

1963–1964

1976

1988

1990

On 16 June, police shoot at an unarmed crowd of children marching in protest in the township of Soweto. Twenty-three people die.

After 27 years, Nelson is released from prison.

Nelson, jointly with South African president, F.W. de Klerk, is awarded the Nobel Peace Prize.

New, free elections are held in South Africa. The ANC wins, and Nelson is elected president.

On 18 July, the United Nations declares Nelson's birthday to be Nelson Mandela International Day in honour of his contributions to peace and human rights.

1993

1994

2004

2009

2013

After many health issues, Nelson formally retires from public life.

Nelson's autobiography, *Long Walk to Freedom*, is published.

On 5 December, at 95 years old, Nelson dies.

Quiz

In what year did Dutch colonizers come to South Africa?

When Nelson borrowed his father's trousers to wear to school, what did he use as a belt to hold them up?

What is the name of Nelson's tribe?

Who was the first white man Nelson shook hands with?

What political group did Nelson join in Johannesburg?

Were white people a majority or a minority in South Africa?

What did Nelson's second wife, Winnie, do for a living when he met her?

Do you remember what you've read?
How many of these questions about
Nelson's life can you answer?

 What is the name of the prison where Nelson served most of his sentence?

 How many years did Nelson spend in prison?

 How old was Nelson when he took office as president of South Africa?

 At what event did Nelson make his last public appearance?

 What name did Nelson's close friends and family call him?

Answers on page 128

Who's who?

Achmat, Zackie
(1962–) South African AIDS and gay rights activist

Annan, Kofi
(1938–2018) United Nations secretary-general from 1997 to 2006

Biko, Steve
(1946–1977) Black People's Convention leader

Botha, P.W.
(1916–2006) prime minister (1978–1984) and then president (1984–1989) of South Africa

Brown, Gordon
(1951–) British prime minister from 2007 to 2010

Bush, George H.W.
(1924–2018) president of the United States from 1989 to 1993

Bush, George W.
(1946–) president of the United States from 2001 to 2009

Castro, Fidel
(1926–2016) Cuban revolutionary and president of Cuba until 2008

Dalindyebo, Jongintaba
(1865–1923) chief who became Nelson's guardian after his father's death

de Klerk, F.W.
(1936–) president of South Africa (1989–1994)

Geldof, Bob
(1951–) Irish singer and political activist

Harris, Reverend Mr
(unknown) headmaster of Clarkebury Boarding Institute

John Paul II
(1920–2005) Pope and head of the Catholic Church from 1978 to 2005

Joyi, Zwelibhangile (swoh-lib-haan-geel)
(unknown) chief who visited the Great Place

Machel, Graça
(1945–) first education minister in free Mozambique, and Nelson's third wife

Mandela, Gadla Henry
(unknown–1930) Nelson's father

Mandela, Nomzamo Winnie Madikizela
(1936–2018) social worker, political activist, and Nelson's second wife

Mandela, Nosekeni Fanny
(unknown–1968) Nelson's mother

Mbeki, Thabo
(1942–) president of South Africa from 1999 to 2008

Mdingane, Miss
(unknown) Nelson's first teacher

Meligqili (mel-leek-qwee-lee)
(unknown) chief who spoke at Nelson's manhood ceremony

Mitterrand, François
(1916–1996) president of France from 1981 to 1995

Nelson, Admiral Lord
(1758–1805) British naval hero

Ntoko Mase, Evelyn
(1922–2004) Nelson's first wife

Sisulu, Walter
(1912–2003) Nelson's friend in the African National Congress, cousin of his first wife

Sofia, Queen
(1938–) queen of Spain

Tambo, Oliver
(1917–1993) Nelson's school friend with whom he started a law firm in 1952

Thatcher, Margaret
(1925–2013) British prime minister from 1979 to 1990

Zuma, Jacob
(1942–) president of South Africa from 2009 to 2018

Glossary

administer
put something into effect, like a law

advised
gave advice to someone

AIDS
infection that attacks the human immune system, which helps keep the body free from infection

ant-heap
hard dirt above an ant colony

apartheid
formal political, social, and economic separation on the basis of race

arranged marriage
parents or guardians pick marriage partners for their children

benefit
something helpful for a person

chasm
deep hole in the earth

chauffeur
professional driver

colonizer
person who creates and controls a new settlement in a foreign land

colony
settlement controlled by a more powerful country

condemnation
strong statement saying that someone or something is wrong

conscience
feeling that you should do the right thing

constitution
set of laws that governs an organization or country

discipline
using self-control to improve your own behaviour

disenchanted
no longer in favour of
something

dispossessed
people who have had land
or belongings taken away
from them

domination
complete control over
someone or something

elite
people of a high class

emancipation
freedom

exile
barred from a country

exploited
person or group used unfairly
by another person or group
for their own advantage

facilities
places built for specific uses

feint
motion used to make an
opponent think you are
attacking one way before
you attack a different way

guardian
person who is responsible
for a child

HIV
virus that causes AIDS

inferior
not as good as something
or someone else

ingrained
hard to change

injustice
unfair act that goes against
someone's rights

instituting
putting into practice or
making into law

insubordination
disobeying an order from
a higher authority

kraal
small farm, with just a
few animals and crops,
that supports a
single family

leprosy
disease in which the body wastes away

logic
organized and reasoned method of thinking about something

magistrate
government official who administers certain laws in a specific area

mythical
imaginary, or from a made-up story

oppress
keep down a certain group of people or a person

parry
defend against a blow by pushing it to the side

peasant
poor farm worker

plowboy (ploughboy)
boy who leads a plough

polio
disease that often leads to loss of movement

political activism
trying to change things in the government

political prisoner
someone in jail because of their political beliefs

prejudice
unfair feeling against certain people or a person

prohibitions
rules that stop people from doing certain things

red tape
lots of unnecessary paperwork demanded by governments or big business

ruthless
without pity, cruel

sabotage
destroy or damage a plan or property

self-sufficient
able to survive on your own

shepherd
person who looks after sheep

significant
important

slingshot
weapon for shooting small stones, made of a V-shaped stick with a handle, and a rubber band. Also called a catapult.

sophisticate
person who knows a lot about world art, culture, and literature

status
social or political position that a person has compared with others

stern
serious in a severe way

strategy
plan

superior
better than something

thatched
made of dried plant material

townships
neighbourhoods in South Africa that were racially segregated during apartheid; only black people lived in townships

transition
change from one state to another

treason
trying to overthrow your country's government

twine
type of string made of two or more strings twisted together

undesirable
person who is not wanted

Index

Rr

red tape 41
retirement 89, 90
rituals 25
Robben Island 60–66
Rolihlahla 8
Rugby World Cup
    87–88

Ss

sabotage 58
schools 16–19, 28–31
self-sufficiency 15
Sharpeville Massacre 53
shirts, Madiba 107
Sisulu, Walter 42–43,
    95, 96
Sofía, queen of
    Spain 94
South Africa 8
Soviet Union 72
Soweto 66–67, 73
sports 31
Springboks 87–88
stick fighting 16
superior 18

Tt

Tambo, Oliver 49–50
Thatcher, Margaret 76
Thembu tribe 8
thinti 16
toothpaste 30

Transkei 9
treason trial 48
trials 48–49, 57–59
tribes 8, 26, 44–45
troublemaker 8
trousers 17

Uu

Union of South Africa 39
United Nations 97, 98
United Nations Security
    Council 69
United States of America
    72
University College of Fort
    Hare 32–34

Vv

voting 40

Ww

water supply 84
Winfrey, Oprah 103

Xx

Xhosa tribe 26

Zz

Zion Christian Church 25
Zuma, Jacob 101

Acknowledgements

DK would like to thank Rebekah Wallin for proofreading; Hilary Bird for the index; Seeta Parmar for additional editorial work; and Victoria Pyke for Anglicization.

The publisher would like to thank the following for their kind permission to reproduce their photographs:
(Key: a-above; b-below/bottom; c-centre; f-far; l-left; r-right; t-top)

9 Alamy Stock Photo: Gallo Images (tr). 11 Alamy Stock Photo: De Luan (c). 21 Getty Images: Matthew Willman / Gallo Images (b). 22 Unity Archives - Moravian Archives Herrnhut. 30 Alamy Stock Photo: GL Archive (bl). 31 iStockphoto.com: Hipokrat (tr). 36 Getty Images: Popperfoto (b). 41 akg-images: Africa Media Online (t). 42 Getty Images: Universal History Archive / UIG (bl). 43 Alamy Stock Photo: Archive PL (c). 45 Getty Images: Hulton-Deutsch Collection / Corbis (c). 48 Rex by Shutterstock: Sipa. 49 Alamy Stock Photo: Peter Jordan (br). 53 akg-images: Africa Media Online (br). 55 Rex by Shutterstock: Sipa. 57 Alamy Stock Photo: Blaine Harrington III (t). 61 Alamy Stock Photo: Robertharding. 63 Getty Images: Dave Hogan (t). 66-67 Getty Images: Bongani Mnguni / City Press / Gallo Images (b). 68 Rex by Shutterstock: (bl). 70 Alamy Stock Photo: Peter Jordan (bl). 72 Getty Images: Trevor Samson / AFP (bl). 74-75 Getty Images: David Turnley / Corbis / VCG. 77 Getty Images: Bernard Bisson / Sygma (tr). 83 Getty Images: Walter Dhladhla / AFP (t); Hanner Frankenfeld / AFP (b). 87 Getty Images: Gary Benard / AFP (t). 89 Getty Images: Odd Andersen / AFP (t). 90 Getty Images: Photofusion / UIG (b). 91 Getty Images: Anna Zieminski / AFP (br).

92 Getty Images: Themba Hadebe / AFP (t). 93 Getty Images: Per-Anders Pettersson (br). 94 Getty Images: Alberto Martin / AFP (tc); Mannie Garcia (cr); Cate Gillon (bc). 99 Getty Images: Pierre-Philippe Marcou / AFP (b); Cameron Spencer (t). 101 Getty Images: Unkel / ullstein bild (tr). 104-105 Getty Images: Erhan Sevenler / Anadolu Agency. 106 Dreamstime.com: Grobler Du Preez. 109 Getty Images: Louise Gubb / Corbis SABA. 111 Getty Images: Chris Jackson (cr)

Cover images: *Front:* Alamy Stock Photo: Interfoto b; *Spine:* Alamy Stock Photo: Interfoto ca

All other images © Dorling Kindersley
For further information see: www.dkimages.com

ANSWERS TO THE QUIZ ON PAGES 116–117

1. 1652; 2. A rope; 3. The Xhosa; 4. Reverend Mr Harris, Clarkebury Boarding Institute Headmaster; 5. The African National Congress (ANC); 6. A minority (always have been); 7. She was a social worker; 8. Robben Island; 9. 27; 10. 77; 11. The football World Cup finals in South Africa in 2010; 12. Madiba